# So God Created You

Written by
**Janis Hanson**

Illustrated by
**Sydney Olmstead**

Digital Design by
**Heather Hanson**

1

ISBN-10: 1494464918
ISBN-13: 978-1494464912

*"You are worthy, our Lord and God, to receive
glory and honor and power, for You created all things,
and by Your will they were created and have their being."*
Revelation 4:11

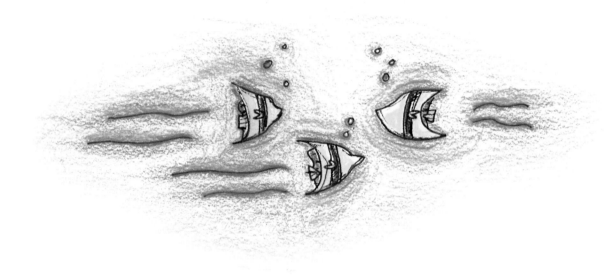

Janis is excited to dedicate this book to
all of her grandchildren.

Sydney would like to dedicate this book
to her husband, Chris and her future children.

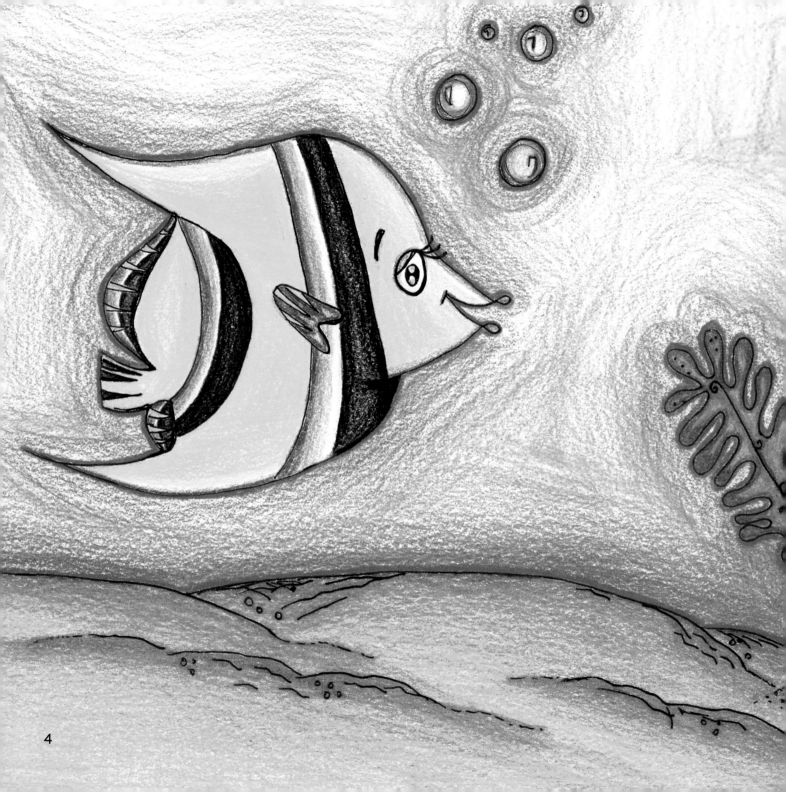

Hi!  I'm an Angelfish.
Isn't that a special name... ANGEL?

Don't you love my beautiful
color?  I'm so bright!

God created me to live underwater.
I get to swim around all the beautiful coral
and green seaweed.

Did you know there is more water to explore than land? From far away the earth looks like a majestic blue marble because most of it is covered by water.

One big thing I cannot do is breathe outside of the water.

So God created me,
He gets to decide.

What if you took me out of the ocean and
put me on the swings or let me go down the slide?

What would happen to me?
EEEK!!!!  I cannot live out of the water.

There are over a million sea creatures and plants that we have seen and discovered but many more millions remain unseen. Only God gets to see them.

Can you see the snail in the cave?

God created the snail with one big "foot like" organ that moves along the surface with a trail of slime.

One thing that a snail cannot do is move fast.  It would take more than a day for a snail to cross a football field and that would be him working at top speed!

So God created him,
He gets to decide.

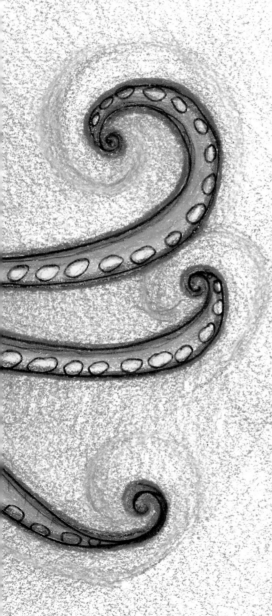

Of all the sea creatures,
the octopus is the most
interesting.  Unlike the snail,
the octopus has eight arms
and no shell.

The octopus may be the
smartest creature in the
sea but it does not live
very long.  Some only live
for six months.

So God created him,
He gets to decide.

Did you know that God created you?
How cool is that!

What is your name?
What is something you can do really well?
What is something you cannot do?

I like how God created
you and I like how
God created me!

When God created you He wrote instructions for you to follow in the book of the Bible.

He asks that you do not lie or steal. He asks that you be kind and obey your parents. He asks that you love God with all your heart. These instructions are for your own good.

So God created you,
He gets to decide.

Would you like to make your own creature?

You get to pick one thing your creature can do
and one thing your creature cannot do.
You create it so you get to decide.

Don't forget to name it!
I like how God created you and
I like how God created me!

Come back and be with me again soon
and you can make another creature.
Just ask for Angel.  See you soon!

Parents, in the back of the book are blank pages for your child to draw their
creatures.  You only need simple art supplies such as crayons, markers and pencils
but if your child is a creative genius you can add paints, glitter or stickers.

Hi, my name is:_____

One thing I can do is:_____

One thing I cannot do is:_____

(You created me, so you get to decide!)

Hi, my name is: _____

One thing I can do is: _____

One thing I cannot do is: _____

(You created me, so you get to decide!)

Hi, my name is:_____

One thing I can do is:_____

One thing I cannot do is:_____

(You created me, so you get to decide!)

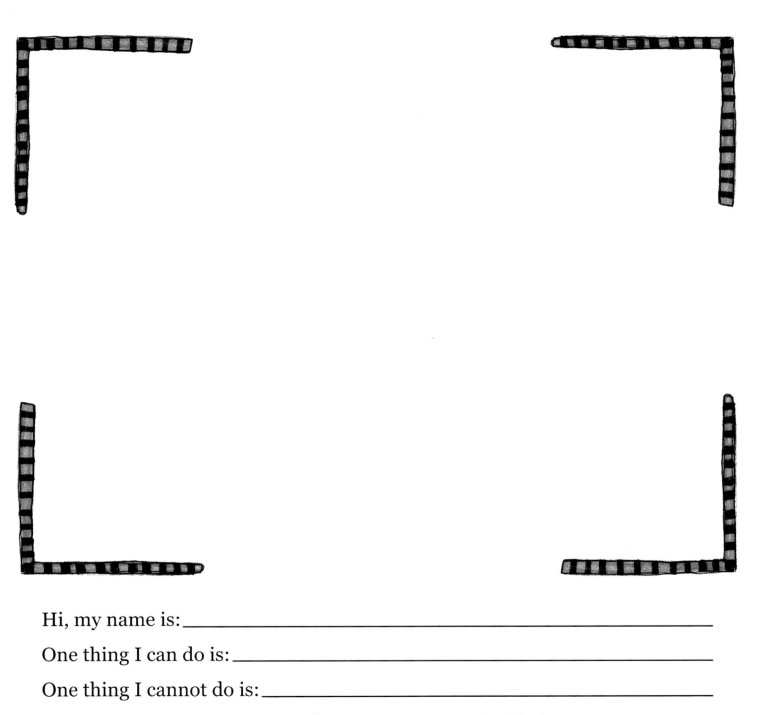

Hi, my name is: _____

One thing I can do is: _____

One thing I cannot do is: _____

(You created me, so you get to decide!)                    25

Hi, my name is: _____

One thing I can do is: _____

One thing I cannot do is: _____

(You created me, so you get to decide!)

Hi, my name is:_____

One thing I can do is:_____

One thing I cannot do is:_____

(You created me, so you get to decide!)

Hi, my name is: _____

One thing I can do is: _____

One thing I cannot do is: _____

(You created me, so you get to decide!)

Hi, my name is: _____

One thing I can do is: _____

One thing I cannot do is: _____

(You created me, so you get to decide!)

Hi, my name is:_____

One thing I can do is:_____

One thing I cannot do is:_____

(You created me, so you get to decide!)

Hi, my name is: _____

One thing I can do is: _____

One thing I cannot do is: _____

(You created me, so you get to decide!)

Hi, my name is: _____

One thing I can do is: _____

One thing I cannot do is: _____

32                    (You created me, so you get to decide!)

Hi, my name is: _____

One thing I can do is: _____

One thing I cannot do is: _____

(You created me, so you get to decide!)

Made in the USA
Columbia, SC
23 October 2018